A CLOSER LOOK BOOK
Published in the United States by
Franklin Watts in 1976

First published in
Great Britain in 1976 by
Hamish Hamilton
Children's Books Ltd,
90 Great Russell Street,
London WC1B 3PT

Designed by David Cook and
Associates and produced by
The Archon Press Ltd,
28 Percy Street,
London W1P 9FF

Printed in Great Britain by
W. S. Cowell Ltd,
Butter Market, Ipswich

Library of Congress
Catalog Card Number: 75–46382
ISBN (Library edition): 0–531–01189–5
ISBN (Trade edition): 0–531–02433–4

The author wishes to
acknowledge the assistance
received from Dr. Jim Flegg,
Director of the British Trust of
Ornithology, Tring,
Hertfordshire, during the
preparation of this book.

A closer LOOK at BIRDS

J. L. Hicks

Illustrated by

John Rignall

Franklin Watts · New York · London · 1976

How birds evolved

The crow-sized *Archaeopteryx,* 150 million years old, is the earliest bird we know.

Ichtyornis, the fish bird, probably fed by grabbing fish from the sea while flying.

A flightless diver, *Hesperornis,* the western bird, had short, flipper-like wings and sharp teeth.

Birds can find food and places to live that earthbound creatures cannot reach. They can also fly away from their enemies. Over the centuries these advantages have fascinated man and have helped birds survive and multiply. Except for fish, birds are the most successful of all the vertebrates, or animals with backbones.

Found nearly everywhere, there are 8,580 different species, or kinds, of birds. Most can fly, many can swim, and others can run very fast. Many birds "sing" beautifully. Some can talk, or at least mimic human speech. Others make no sound at all. They can weigh anywhere from ⅓ ounce to 300 pounds. Yet there is one thing that makes a bird a bird: feathers. A large bird such as a swan may have 25,000 feathers. But even the smallest sparrow has 3,500!

Feathers also tell us something about where birds came from. They evolved (developed) from reptiles. A study of fossils (parts or impressions of plants or animals preserved in the earth's crust) shows that feathers developed from scales, which covered these early reptiles. Birds still have some of the scales left on their feet and legs.

In the age of dinosaurs, 200 million years ago, some reptiles became gliders, as their front legs developed into wings. Skin grew over what once had been toes. Some of these pterosaurs, or winged lizards, grew to tremendous size. But they could not be called birds simply because they could fly. Some birds cannot fly, and various other animals (insects, for example) can.

A link between flying reptiles and birds was found when a fossil turned up in Germany in 1861. The 150-million-year-old animal had sharp teeth and a long, bony tail. In all ways, it had been a reptile—but it had feathers. Scientists named it *Archaeopteryx,* meaning "ancient wing."

Though *Archaeopteryx* was the first bird, it did not have strong muscles for flying. It did have three claws on each wing and probably used them to climb trees and glide from branch to branch. From other fossils, scientists know of two other early birds: *Ichtyornis,* a fish-eater, and *Hesperornis,* the non-flying western bird with short, penguin-like flippers.

These three ancient birds had little more in common than feathers. The same is true of many birds today.

Parts of a bird

All birds have feathers—down feathers for warmth, contour feathers for shape, and flight feathers for flying. The flight feathers are made of a light, rigid shaft, with small parallel barbs on each side, where tiny side branches, or barbules, begin. Each barbule has even smaller branches called barbicels; shaped like hooks or notches, they lock the barbules together, making the whole feather into a surface that is both light and strong.

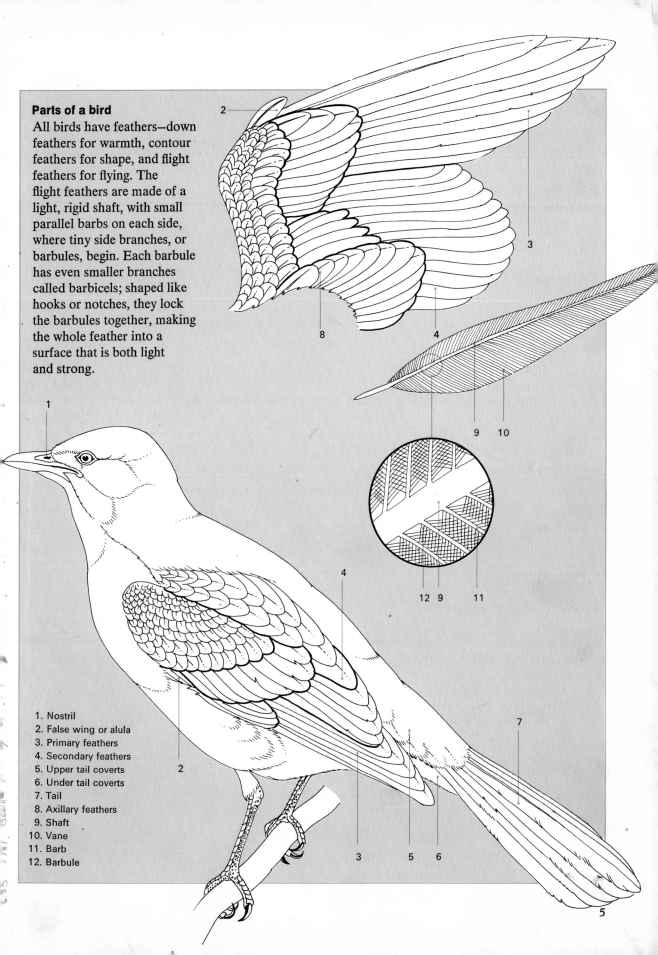

1. Nostril
2. False wing or alula
3. Primary feathers
4. Secondary feathers
5. Upper tail coverts
6. Under tail coverts
7. Tail
8. Axillary feathers
9. Shaft
10. Vane
11. Barb
12. Barbule

Flying

Birds—the 100,000 million of them—owe their great success to their ability to fly. Flight lets them feed where many other animals cannot. They can get away from enemies, settle new areas, and move whenever food becomes hard to find and the climate unfavorable.

The key to a bird's ability to fly is its feathers. Feathers are strong enough to lift the bird, yet light enough to bend with the wind, helping it move easily through air.

Further, flying uses a lot of energy. To burn up food and change it quickly to energy, birds have high body temperatures, about 104° F. Their hearts beat fast, and they breathe quickly, taking in oxygen through both the lungs and extra air sacs. To keep it light, a bird's skeleton is made of small, round, hollow bones, except for the breast, or "keel" bone, to which are attached breast muscles, the heaviest part of the bird. These must be large and strong since they move the bird's wings up and down.

Landing and braking
Its body nearly erect, feet forward, a puffin spreads its wings and tail to slow down. A false wing, called an alula, is raised to control air flowing over the wings.

Upstroke and downstroke
Birds fly by beating their wings down and up; the downstroke is the power stroke. The wings are held stiff, primary feathers locking together to form a large surface for the air below. The wings beat down and forward and are lifted by air rising up. On the upstroke, the wings are curved so that air flows over them easily, and they form a small surface to air coming down from above. The primaries separate and twist to make the wing easier to lift. At the top of the upstroke they lock together, ready for the downstroke.

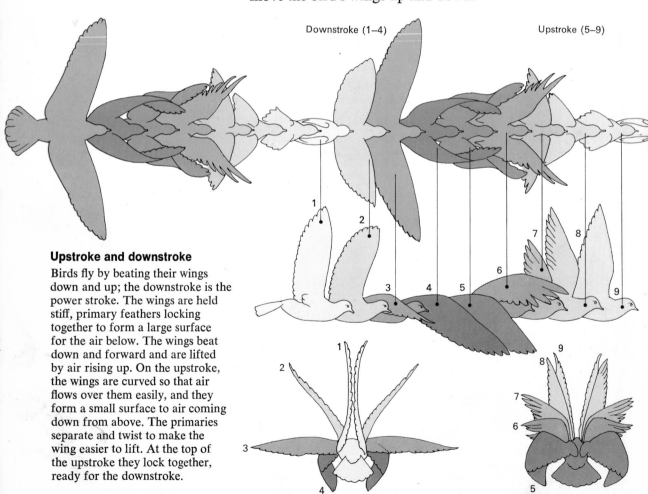

Downstroke (1–4)   Upstroke (5–9)

Starting and Stopping

To take off, a bird leans forward, bends its legs, spreads its wings, and jumps into the air. Once up, it brings its wings down to fly. To land, it pulls itself upright, stretches its legs toward the perch, and beats its wings against the wind.

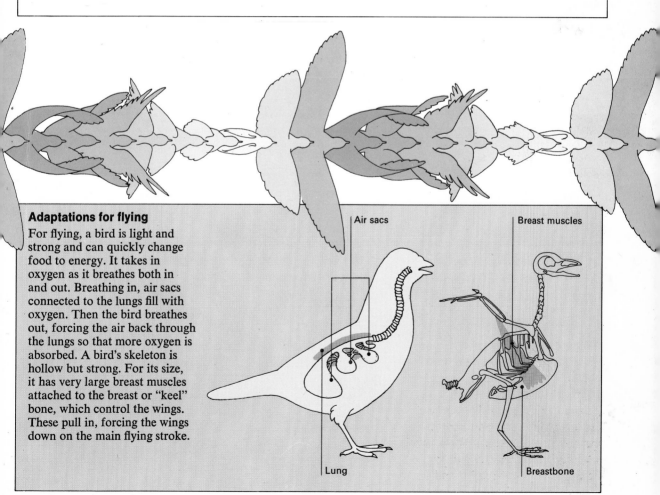

Adaptations for flying

For flying, a bird is light and strong and can quickly change food to energy. It takes in oxygen as it breathes both in and out. Breathing in, air sacs connected to the lungs fill with oxygen. Then the bird breathes out, forcing the air back through the lungs so that more oxygen is absorbed. A bird's skeleton is hollow but strong. For its size, it has very large breast muscles attached to the breast or "keel" bone, which control the wings. These pull in, forcing the wings down on the main flying stroke.

Air sacs

Breast muscles

Lung

Breastbone

Ways of flying

Wing shape tells a lot about a bird's way of flying. Eagles soar for hours without beating their long, broad wings, though they can be powerful fliers. Swifts fly rapidly on narrow, pointed wings. Birds who feed on the ground or water have short wings, easy to fold away. A duck's short, broad wings weigh over twice the long, narrow wings of a shearwater. Thus the duck must flap its wings quickly to carry its weight. Birds also help each other fly. A goose flying in a V formation is lifted by wind produced by the bird ahead.

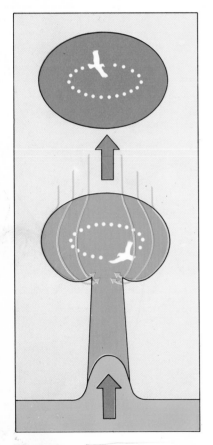

Thermal soaring
Hot air rises, and a thermal is a column of warm air that rises over warm ground. Cold air, streaming down each side, causes a floating bubble to form. Pelicans and eagles, which have long, broad wings, ride a thermal, circling in the warm air with wings extended so that it carries them up.

Brown pelican

Eagle

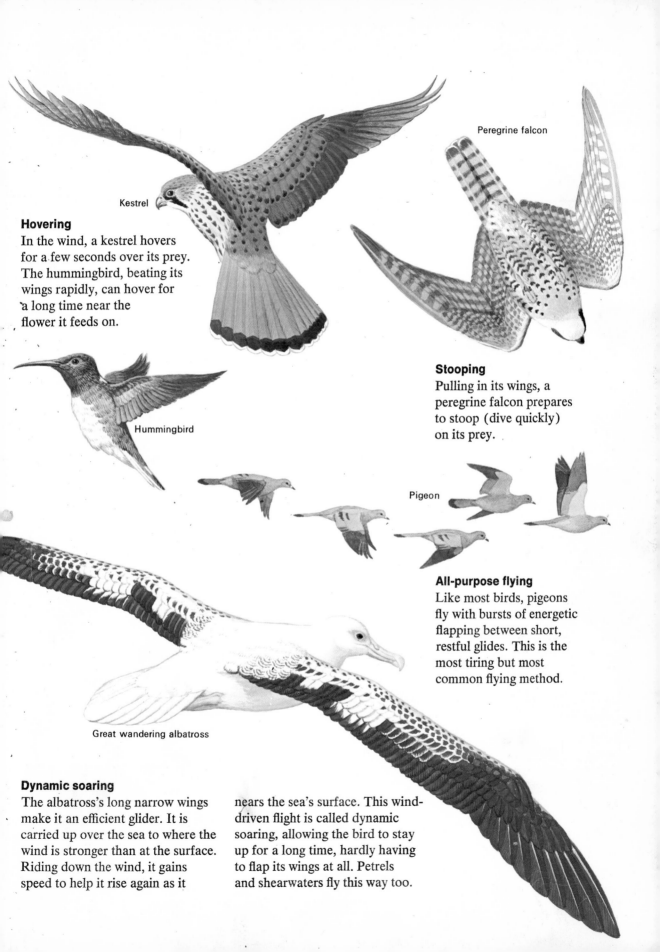

Peregrine falcon

Kestrel

Hovering
In the wind, a kestrel hovers for a few seconds over its prey. The hummingbird, beating its wings rapidly, can hover for a long time near the flower it feeds on.

Hummingbird

Stooping
Pulling in its wings, a peregrine falcon prepares to stoop (dive quickly) on its prey.

Pigeon

All-purpose flying
Like most birds, pigeons fly with bursts of energetic flapping between short, restful glides. This is the most tiring but most common flying method.

Great wandering albatross

Dynamic soaring
The albatross's long narrow wings make it an efficient glider. It is carried up over the sea to where the wind is stronger than at the surface. Riding down the wind, it gains speed to help it rise again as it nears the sea's surface. This wind-driven flight is called dynamic soaring, allowing the bird to stay up for a long time, hardly having to flap its wings at all. Petrels and shearwaters fly this way too.

Birds that cannot fly

People once thought that flightless birds were simply evolving slower than flying ones—that their wings were still developing. We now know that though these birds could once fly, they have lost the ability.

Birds lose the ability either because something is gained by adapting the wings to do another job, or because flight is no longer needed. Flippers, more useful than wings to the fish-eating Antarctic penguin, evolved in their place. Other birds, though giving up flight, did not develop new skills. Some species settled islands where there were no predators (animals who kill for food); with no need to escape, there was no need to fly.

Large earthbound species are called ratites, from the Latin word for raft, a small boat with no keel. They lack both the keel-like breastbone and the flight muscles usually attached to it. But these birds developed in other ways: a huge ostrich can run 35 miles per hour and kick hard.

The diatryma

Over 6 feet tall and a meat-eater only, the diatryma had a head as long as a horse. It also had thick, strong legs and probably chased small mammals and reptiles.

Rhea 4 feet 4 ins.
South America

Emu 6 feet
Australia

King penguin 3 feet
Subantarctic islands

Adelie penguin 2 feet 4 ins.
Antarctica

Kakapo 2 feet 1 in.
New Zealand

Takahe 2 feet 1 in.
New Zealand

The price to pay

The New Zealand moa, 13 feet tall and weighing nearly 50 pounds, and the shorter but heavier elephant bird of Madagascar are both now extinct. They traded flight for size, a good defense until the coming of humans. Two flightless sea birds are also now extinct: the dodo and the great auk. They were easy prey for the settlers of the islands on which they lived.

Moa
New Zealand

Dodo
Indian Ocean

Elephant bird
Madagascar

Great auk
North Atlantic

Ostrich 7 feet 5 ins.
Africa

Cassowary 5 feet
Australia and
New Guinea

Kiwi 1 foot 8 ins.
New Zealand

Flightless cormorant 3 feet
Galapagos Islands

The variety of birds

When ornithologists, or bird observers, group together birds to classify them, they consider features such as foot shape and how birds get food. They also study fossils to see which birds are close and which are only distant relatives.

Birds are vertebrates of the class Aves, meaning simply "birds"; only feathered animals belong. They are divided into 27 orders, the orders into 155 families, the families into groups called genera, and the genera into 8,580 species.

Orders

There are 27 orders of birds. A typical representative of each is illustrated below, and the numbers in parentheses indicate the number of species in each order.

Apterygiformes Kiwis (3)

Struthioniformes Ostriches (1)

Casuariiformes Emus (4)

Rheiformes Rheas (2)

Podicipediformes Grebes (17)

Procellariiformes Albatrosses (81)

Sphenisciformes Penguins (15)

Gaviiformes Divers (4)

Pelecaniformes Pelicans (50)

Ciconiiformes Herons (117)

Anseriformes Ducks (149)

Falconiformes Birds of prey (274)

Galliformes Game birds (250)

Gruiformes Cranes (185)

Charadriiformes Gulls (293)

Columbiformes Pigeons (301)

Psittaciformes Parrots (317)

Cuculiformes Cuckoos (143)

Strigiformes Owls (132)

Tinamiformes Tinamous (42)

Caprimulgiformes Frogmouths (92)

Apodiformes Hummingbirds (388)

Trogoniformes Trogons (35)

Coliiformes Colies (6)

Coraciiformes Kingfishers (192)

Piciformes Woodpeckers (377)

Passeriformes Thrushes (5,110)

Crested curassow
The family Cracidae

Vulturine guinea fowl
The family Numididae

Hoatzin
The family Opisthocomidae

Families

Orders are divided into families. The seven families of the order Galliformes include game birds, domestic chickens, and turkeys.

Mallee fowl
The family Megapodiidae

Lady Amherst pheasant
The family Phasianidae

North American turkey
The family Meleagrididae

Red grouse
The family Tetraonidae

Species

The turkey family, Meleagrididae, of the order Galliformes, contains two species.

The ocellated turkey
The rarer species is a brilliantly colored native of South America.

The North American turkey
This is the more common species. Raised for food, it is also seen in the wild.

Beaks for feeding

Food is energy. Because they need so much energy, birds eat a lot. Some eat equal to 30 percent of their body weight each day.

Every bird has a beak suited to handle the food it eats. In the early stages of development, only those beaks shaped to deal with available food became lasting features. Often a beak limits a bird to one food source. Some finches were born with the tips of their beaks crossed. Though many starved, others survived because only they could draw out seeds from pine cones. These birds bred, and their crossed-beak young survived too. A new species had been established. There are many such examples.

In some cases, different birds evolved similar beaks. American hummingbirds, Australian honey eaters, and African sunbirds, though not of the same family, all developed long, pointed beaks and tongues for sucking nectar from flowers. Luckily, the long distances between their homes make a fight over the blossoms unnecessary.

Digging for insects
The woodpecker finch of the Galapagos Islands is, we think, the only bird that really uses tools. It draws out grubs and insects from holes by stabbing them with a thorn or a spike held in its beak.

The egg fancier
Eggs are important in the diet of the scavenging Egyptian vulture. It picks up small eggs in its beak and breaks them by dropping them to the ground. With ostrich eggs, since the egg is too large to pick up, the vulture takes a stone in its beak and drops it on the egg.

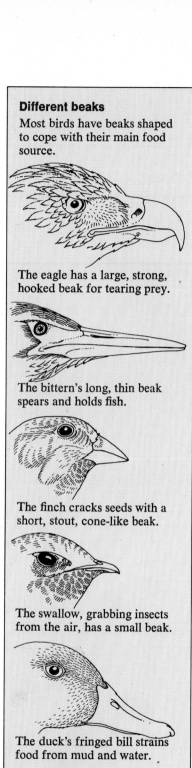

Different beaks

Most birds have beaks shaped to cope with their main food source.

The eagle has a large, strong, hooked beak for tearing prey.

The bittern's long, thin beak spears and holds fish.

The finch cracks seeds with a short, stout, cone-like beak.

The swallow, grabbing insects from the air, has a small beak.

The duck's fringed bill strains food from mud and water.

The sunbird gets nectar from flowers through its narrow bill.

Ways of feeding

Swifts and swallows (1) catch insects while flying with their narrow beaks wide open. A skimmer (2) "plows" the water for fish with the lower half of its long, narrow beak. The flamingo*(3) filters mud with a device at the edge of its mouth, whereas the upcurving bill of the avocet (4) skims the surface slime.

Eyes and ears

Owls are super night hunters. Though an owl's sight at night is much better than ours, its skill comes from its sharp hearing. Even in the pitch-dark an owl can locate its prey and pounce, silently swooping down on its victim.

But for most birds sight is the more useful sense. Birds see well and, for their size, their eyes are large. Most have eyes on each side of the head, giving them a wide field of vision. A duck, for one, can see all around without turning its head. But using only one eye, a bird cannot tell how far away an object is. To judge distance it focuses both eyes on the object and looks at it from several angles, frequently cocking its head. We cannot judge distance with only one eye either, but both our eyes are in front so we do not have to move our heads. Predatory birds have forward-facing eyes too; as soon as they sight their prey, they know how far away it is.

Birds' eyeballs are flatter than ours; all objects, near or far, are in focus at the same time. If we look at something close, objects far away grow blurry. The same thing happens to objects nearby when we focus on something far away.

Ears and nose

On the bald condor, the ears—holes in back of the head—and the nostrils—near the base of the beak—can be clearly seen. The ears and nostrils of most birds are usually hidden by feathers.

Other senses

A sharp sense of smell is not very important to most birds. But the kiwi, who has poor sight, finds worms with nostrils at the tip of its long bill. The turkey buzzard is also known to have sharp smell and, it is said, can smell dead animals from high above, even if they are hidden. The snipe, however, hunts for food by touch, pushing its long, flexible beak into the mud until it feels a worm. Oilbirds use sound to fly through the caves where they nest. As they enter, they make clicking noises; the echo produced tells them how close they are to the walls and to the nest area.

Oilbird

Kiwi

Turkey buzzard

Snipe

A swampland community

The birds of the Everglades show how different feet serve different purposes. The claws of the swallow-tailed kite (1) pluck fish from the water. The ivory-billed woodpecker (2) grips firmly to a tree while drilling. The great blue heron (3) wades on its long legs with toes spread out so it won't sink in the mud. A pair of cinnamon teals (4, 5) and a wood duck (6) move easily along on webbed feet, and a purple gallinule (7) swims with its long, flapping toes. Ground-living birds like the common snipe (8) and the sora rail (9) have strong legs for running. The anhinga (10) has all four toes in front, united by a web to make it strong for swimming. On slender reeds, a Bachman's sparrow (11) and a red-winged blackbird (12) cling with grasping toes. The strangest feet of all are the lily-trotter's (13), who can walk over floating leaves on its long, thin, spidery toes.

Different feet

In their development, birds' legs and feet became specialized. The three basic feet types show this: perching feet with toes that curl; long, straight-toed feet for walking or wading; and webbed or flapped feet for swimming.

There are many variations within these three types, even in the number of toes. Most birds have four or three, but a few have only two. To perch, some have three in front and one behind. Tree-climbing woodpeckers, with two in front and two behind, can cling to trees better. Eagles' feet are perfect for carrying off slain prey, and with the toothed comb on its toe a heron grooms its feathers.

But problems do result from overspecialization: able fliers, like swifts and frigate birds, can hardly walk. The swift's feet are suited only for perching. And the frigate bird, a coast-dweller, cannot swim, its legs too weak and the toe webbing too small. Penguins, who swim at 20 miles per hour, waddle clumsily on land. At times they stop struggling and belly-flop to the ground, pushing themselves along the ice with their flippers. Other swimmers, such as grebes and divers, can hardly move at all on shore. But most species can get around on land.

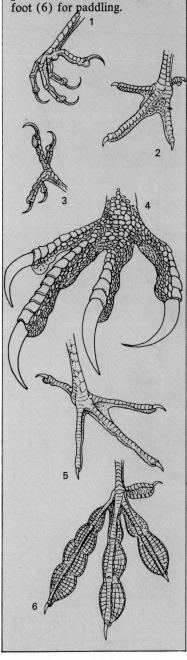

Different kinds of feet
Birds have feet suited for many things: the passerine foot (1) for perching on twigs; the grouse foot (2) for running; the woodpecker foot (3) for clinging; the predator's foot (4) for holding prey; the heron's foot (5) to prevent sinking; and the grebe's foot (6) for paddling.

Colors to blend

Flash patterns

Plovers have a good defense against enemies: patterns that appear on their wings only when they are flying. When they land and fold their wings, the patterns disappear, confusing predators who might be following the markings.

Ducks and drakes

In water, a drake will display colorful plumage. The duck is in more danger; because she guards the nest, she has drab, camouflaging feathers. This difference between the sexes is called sexual dimorphism.

Colors either hide a bird or make it easy to see, and provide effective camouflage for many species. One common disguise is countershading. The bird's feathers are darker on top than below. Since more light comes from above, the bird seems evenly shaded and is less easily seen. Even better is a design that blends with the bird's background. The wader's mottled brown and white back makes it look like a heap of pebbles to predators. And camouflage can hide predators themselves. Some owls, standing perfectly still, look exactly like a stump of a broken tree branch. Bold, striped patterns that distort a bird's real shape are another effective form of camouflage.

By contrast, birds traveling in flocks are often colored to attract attention. These birds are meant to be spotted by others of the same species, for bright plumage in the male is important for mating. No other animals show such range in color and beauty, going from drab to gaudy.

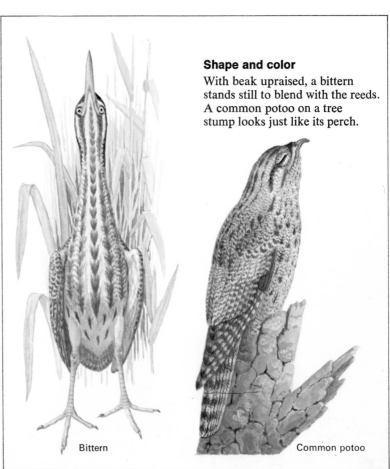

Shape and color

With beak upraised, a bittern stands still to blend with the reeds. A common potoo on a tree stump looks just like its perch.

Bittern

Common potoo

The snowy owl
Against the ice and snow of the Arctic, the snowy owl is almost invisible. It does not change its plumage in summer to match its surroundings. This may be because it is a predator and has no need to protect itself this way.

Courtship and display

The bird you hear sing each day in spring is making a claim. It can be a warning to others of its species not to enter its territory. Birds who eat different food may share the area, but if one of the same species approaches, the owner will threaten angrily by lifting its wings. A male newcomer may fight if he wants the space, but a female come to share the territory will quickly submit. Singing that warns off rivals also attracts a mate.

Birds communicate by voice and movement. Each species has its own method: this is vital in mating season since some species look alike. Birds warn each other of danger. Nestlings ask to be fed, and hens tell their young where they are. But the most interesting bird conversation is that of courtship. It is called display, and its rituals can be complex. A crane bows to a female and then jumps up and down until she joins in the dance. Males, or cocks, proudly show off their splendid plumage. A peacock rattles his rainbow-hued tail; the blue bird of paradise hangs upside down till his plumes fall into their most stunning pattern. Some birds make other noises: the golden-collared manakin "snaps" his wings, and the grouse beats his in steady drum rolls.

A few species, like the swan, choose a lifelong mate. But most cocks mate with many hens, taking no part in raising the families that result.

Different colors

One form of sexual dimorphism (see page 20) is shown in the eclectus parrot of Indonesia. The female is red with blue markings, the male green with red sides.

Birds of paradise

The great bird of paradise dances with other males, on a tree. When a female approaches, they immediately stop moving and wait while she selects a mate.

Blue-footed boobies

These South American seabirds act out a strange, formal, display dance before they mate. The male begins by showing off his bright blue feet.

He parades with his head up while the female bows.

He displays, head up and wings wide open.

The female answers by flapping her wings and raising her head.

The pair then walk away, bowing to each other. Soon after, they mate.

Courtship rituals

Courtship brings birds together, even if only for a short time. Their ways of courting are like some of ours.

Singing

A thrush sings to attract a mate and to warn off rivals from his territory.

Ritual feeding

A roseate tern gives a fish to his mate. This is a way to get the female to start laying eggs.

Building

A male bower bird builds a shelter of twigs and shells to attract a mate.

A ruffs' "lek"

A lek is the area in which ruffs meet during mating season. The cocks open out their ruffs, or feathers, pose, dance, and put on mock fights, which can become real. The females, called reeves, wait to mate with whichever male seems strongest.

23

Nest building

Birds do not *decide* to build nests for their eggs. Temperature changes and more daylight hours set off the instinctive behavior. Any bird, even a bird who never saw a nest, can build one just like those of its ancestors.

The cup-shaped nest of leaves, grass, twigs, and feathers is the most common type, but many birds such as the rufous ovenbird use stones and mud. Swifts use their saliva, which hardens when exposed to air; the tailor bird sews leaves together to form a hanging pocket; and the eagle erects a high fortress of branches. The emperor penguin already has a nest: the father's feet. Placed on them when laid, the single egg is covered by skin hanging from the bird's belly. The male stands for two months through the icy Antarctic winter until the egg hatches, when he will have lost 30 percent of his weight!

However varied the nests, all are designed for one purpose: to safely house the eggs which contain the young.

The tailor bird
This bird's nest is leaves "sewn" together with plant fibers.

The goldcrest's nest
The goldcrest, only 3½ inches long and Europe's smallest bird, makes a nest of moss and cobwebs that hangs from the thin upper branches of a fir tree.

The sociable weaver

Weavers build nests by knotting grass together, holding down one end with a foot while they tie the knot with their beaks and the other foot. South Africa's sociable weavers build a roof together, often a very large one. Each pair then makes its own nest, like a hanging basket, below. Up to 100 pairs work together this way.

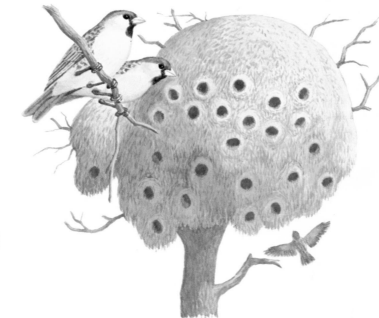

Someone else's nest

Some species, known as brood parasites, rely on others to raise their young. The European cuckoo chooses a nest, waits until it has eggs, then lays one of her own, tossing out some of the nest eggs to make room for hers. Although much larger, the cuckoo egg usually looks like the host's eggs. The cuckoo chick hatches after about 12 days. A sensitive spot on its back makes the chick react to any object it touches, and it pushes the other nestlings and eggs out of the nest. The cuckoo is then raised alone. The American cowbird acts in a similar way, though the chick does not throw out its nest-mates, but is raised with them. Though naked, blind, and helpless when it hatches, the African honey guide chick has sharp, fang-like hooks on its beak. It uses them to kill its nest-mates. After a few days, the hooks drop off, and the chick is raised by the host.

Cuckoo   Cowbird   Honey guide

Cuckoo egg   Meadow bunting egg   Honey guide chick

Cuckoo in the nest

Eggs and hatching

Females start egg-laying often the day after the nest is done, and produce one a day in many species, though fewer in others. Larger birds take longer to form the egg. Clutch size (total number of eggs) can tell us about a bird's chances in life. The albatross, who may live quite long, lays only one egg, while ducks, more popular prey, can lay 20. Some birds will not replace any lost or stolen eggs, but others, like the domestic hen, will.

Eggs need heat for the life within to grow. A sitting bird develops a brood patch on its breast: feathers fall out, blood flows to the area, the temperature rises, and the eggs are warmed. Incubation periods (time until the eggs hatch) vary, about 2 weeks for finches, 12 for albatrosses. Most birds start incubating after all the eggs are laid; but some, like the barn owl, begin on each egg right away. If food is scarce, owlets hatched later may starve or be eaten by nest-mates. This ensures survival of at least a few.

Protected eggs
The song thrush's eggs, laid in a nest, do not need camouflage.

Patterned eggs
The plover's eggs, lying on a beach, are colored like pebbles.

The variety of eggs
Egg size depends on the size of the hen and the type of chick. Nidifugous chicks, which develop more before hatching, have large eggs to hold the extra food they need. The eggs shown are drawn to scale and show the differences in shape, color, and pattern. In general, eggs laid in a hidden nest—like the owl's—are plain and round, while those laid in the open blend with their surroundings. The ostrich lays the largest egg, the hummingbird the smallest.

Owl

Hummingbird

Guillemot

Great black-backed gull

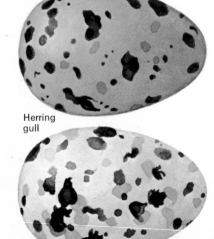

Herring gull

Crested tinamou

Ostrich

The developing egg

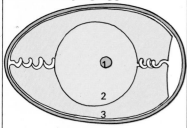

The embryo (1) gets food from the yolk (2) and warmth from the albumen, or white (3). Oxygen comes through the pores in the eggshell.

Blood vessels develop to carry the food from the yolk to the growing embryo.

Shortly before hatching, an egg tooth grows on the chick's beak, and cheeping can be heard through the shell.

The chick uses the egg tooth, which it later sheds, to break the shell open.

The mallee fowl

Australia's male mallee fowl makes as a nest a pile of rotting leaves and sand. The hen approaches the pile only to lay her eggs, which incubate in the heat given off by the rotting mixture. The male spends five hours a day keeping the temperature about 90° F., testing it with his tongue. If it gets too warm, he takes away the sand; if it is too cold, he adds some. The chicks, who dig themselves out, are completely free and never see their parents.

Different chicks

There are two kinds of newly hatched chicks. Those called nidifugous ("fleeing from the nest") are hatched ready to face the world. They can see, walk, and even feed themselves. Nidiculous ("remaining in the nest") chicks are hatched blind, featherless, and completely dependent on their parents.

Caring for the brood

Nidifugous chick
A young pheasant chick stands motionless at its mother's warning signal.

Birds are attentive parents, making sure their young are well fed, warm, and trained to cope with life alone. But the two basic types of young bird—nidifugous and nidiculous—need very different amounts of care. The pheasant, a nidifugous species, after only a few hours of life is alert and feathered and can walk about. Game birds, most waterfowl, waders, and chickens are also nidifugous.

Nidiculous birds include songbirds, crows, and parrots. Days after hatching, the naked chicks, their eyes tightly closed, cannot even roll over. They merely eat and foul the nest. The parents must clean the nest and keep the chicks warm by brooding (covering them with their bodies) or they would die of cold. They demand a lot of food; songbirds may have to make 40 trips an hour, bringing back insects to satisfy the chicks.

But this does not last long. By eating a lot, they grow rapidly, often maturing while nidifugous chicks are still infants. In two weeks, parents may lure or trick them into leaving the nest. They are then taught to feed themselves and to fly properly, though some chicks will have exercised their wings and can already fly. A few more weeks and the young birds depart forever, leaving the parents to settle down to raise another brood.

Penguin nurseries
Emperor penguins live in large groups and together care for their young. The down-covered chicks gather in large groups, or nurseries. A few adults stay behind to guard them while the others go off to find them food.

Rearing

Four species of birds show the differences in care needed by young birds. Most able to cope is the mallee fowl chick. It digs itself out of its nest and can take care of itself from the very first day, never seeing its parents. The pochard duckling, within a few hours of hatching, can swim and dive for weeds and insects underwater. Ducklings stay near their mother, who for comfort occasionally broods them, but they can survive even when left alone the day they hatch. Bullfinch chicks are nidiculous and need constant care during the first weeks of life. The parent feeds its chicks insects and seeds, shoving them into ever-open mouths. This can go on for up to 16 days. By this time, the chicks have grown feathers and are learning how to fly and get their own food.

Mallee fowl

Pochard duck

Bullfinch

Processed food

Brown pelicans also have nidiculous chicks, but feed them in a different way. The parent catches fish, often flying far to get it, and half digests it. When the bird returns to the nest, the chick reaches far into its parent's throat to eat the fish that has been brought back up from the stomach. The adult's stomach juices are mixed with the fish to help the chick digest the food. This kind of feeding can last for two months, and a growing pelican can eat up to 150 pounds of this partly digested meal before leaving the nest.

Brown pelican

Migration

Twice a year, millions of birds set off on journeys called migrations. They fly south, before winter robs them of food, and return to the breeding grounds in spring. Many do not survive the trip. They are killed by storms, accidents, hunger, and predators. Why do they go? Because they must: food supplies at home are not adequate. Even though there are problems, the trip is worthwhile.

How do birds find their way? How can a young cuckoo, migrating a month after the adult birds, find its way to a place where it has never been? How do birds know when to start eating high-energy food to prepare for their journey? How do they know when to start?

We don't know. Perhaps they follow the sun and stars, using them as sailors use instruments. Perhaps they have built-in "biological clocks." Someday we will discover the answers. Until we do, the mystery of migration remains only one fascinating aspect of the world of birds.

Hibernation

Poor-wills are the only birds we know of that hibernate (sleep through winter). Found in the Colorado Desert, they pass the foodless winter among the rocks. Their heartbeat and breathing become barely noticeable, and their body temperature drops.

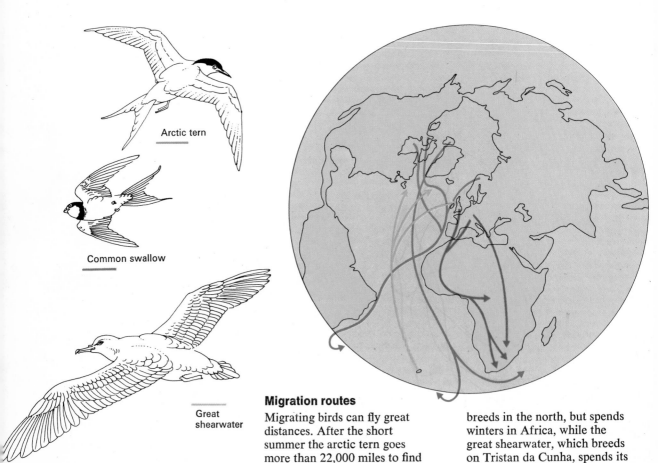

Arctic tern

Common swallow

Great shearwater

Migration routes

Migrating birds can fly great distances. After the short summer the arctic tern goes more than 22,000 miles to find food. The common swallow breeds in the north, but spends winters in Africa, while the great shearwater, which breeds on Tristan da Cunha, spends its winters in the north.

Cranes

For centuries people have noted the migration of cranes. The Bible says, "Cranes keep the time of their coming." The ancient Greeks timed their fall plowing by the birds' flight south. These large, graceful birds became a symbol or sign of spring and good luck to some, trouble to others.